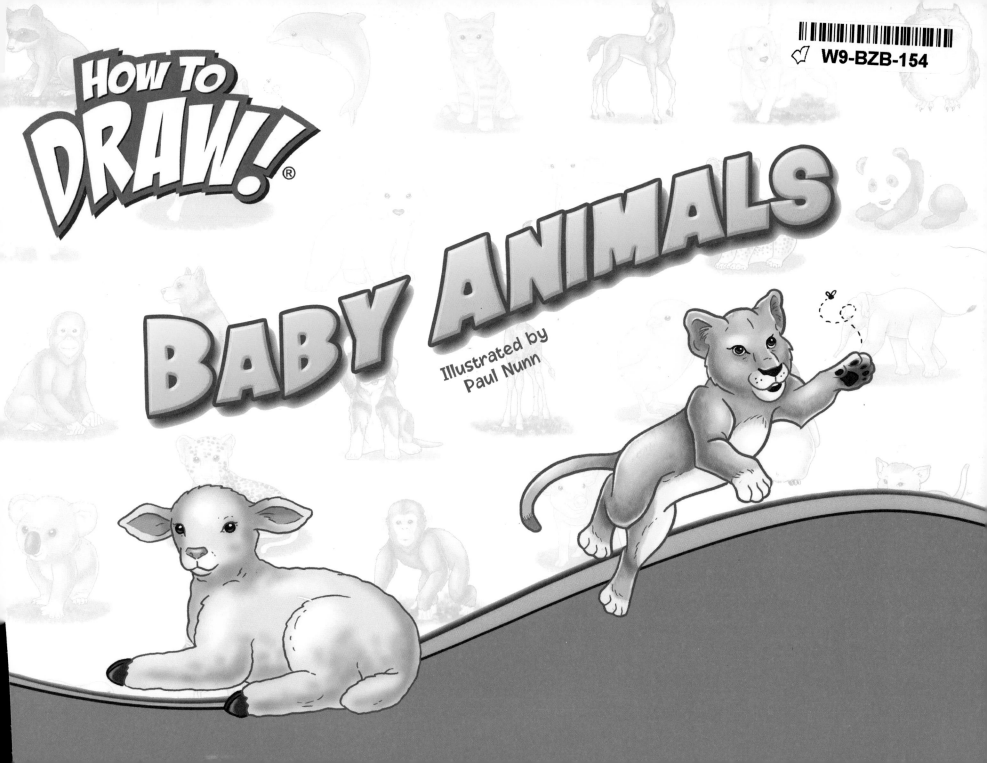

How To DRAW!®

BABY ANIMALS

Illustrated by
Paul Nunn

SUPPLIES

- NUMBER 2 PENCILS
- SOFT ERASER
- COLORED PENCILS
- MARKERS OR CRAYONS

HELPFUL HINTS

1. Take your time with steps 1 and 2.
Following the first steps carefully will make the final steps easier. The first two steps create a foundation of the figure—much like the frame of a house forms the foundation of the rest of the building. Next comes the fun part: creating the smooth, clean outline drawing of the animal and adding all the finishing touches, details, shading, and color.

2. Always keep your pencil lines light and soft.
This will make your guidelines easier to erase when you no longer need them.

3. Don't be afraid to erase.
It usually takes a lot of drawing and erasing before you will be satisfied with the way your drawing looks.

4. Add details at the end.
Shading and finishing touches should be the last step *after* you have blended and refined all the shapes.

5. Remember: Practice makes perfect.
Don't be discouraged if you don't get the hang of it right away. Just keep drawing, erasing, and redrawing until you do.

Polar Bear Cub

A polar bear cub is very tiny when born, weighing no more than one pound. It lives with its mother until the age of two years—that's when the cub is ready to hunt and survive all on its own.

1 Begin by drawing these circular shapes for the polar bear's head and body. The bear's muzzle starts out as a perfect oval and will be refined later.

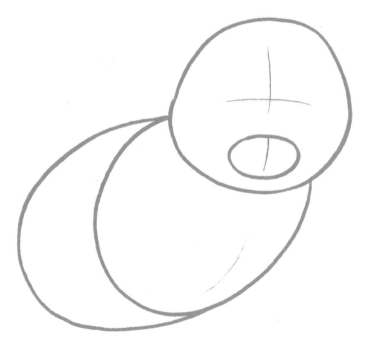

2 Next, pencil in the rough shapes for the legs and ears. Keep your drawings light. Once you are happy with the main form, you can begin to add details like the eyes, mouth, and nose.

Now that your polar bear has really taken shape, you can tighten it up by adding fine details like fur, whiskers, and nails.

4 Your drawing looks great! You can finish it off by adding some color and shading. Your polar bear cub is ready to play in the Arctic snow.

African Elephant Calf

An African elephant calf weighs about 250 pounds at birth. This calf can stand within an hour of being born, and is able to walk along with its mother and the herd just a few days later. In a few months, the calf learns how to use its trunk really well. By the time a calf becomes an adult, it can weigh more than 10,000 pounds.

2 Add long legs to the body. We will draw this elephant making a long stride. Next, add the ear, tail, and tubular trunk.

1 Start by sketching a slanted oval for its head, then draw a larger shape for its body, as shown. Note the curve of its back.

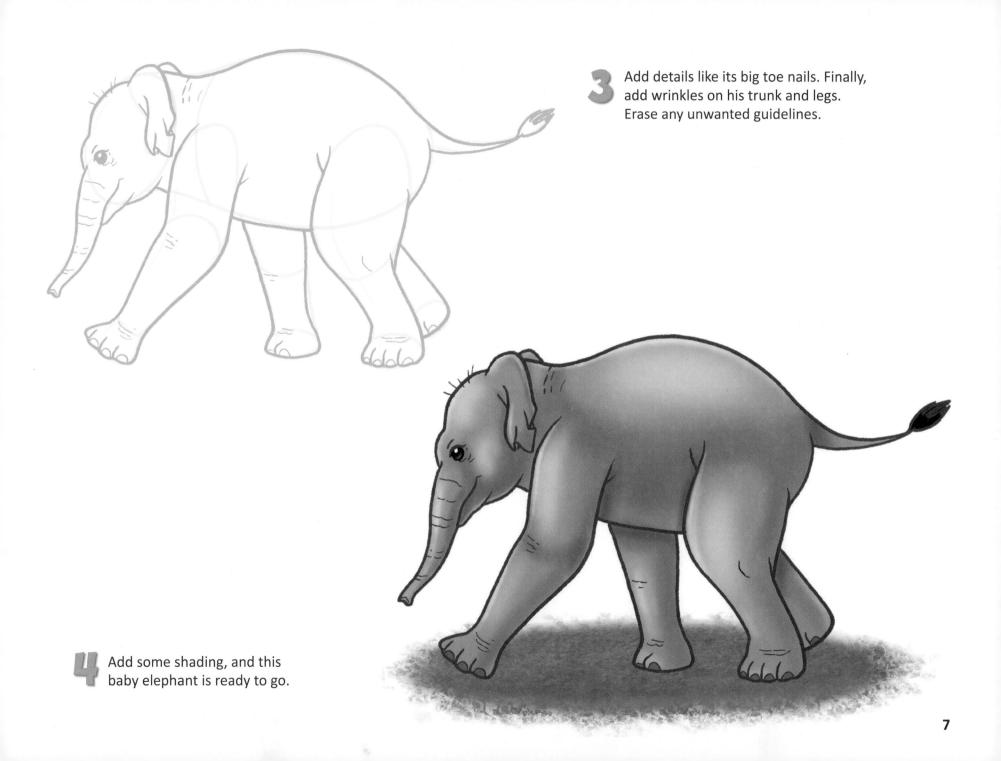

3 Add details like its big toe nails. Finally, add wrinkles on his trunk and legs. Erase any unwanted guidelines.

4 Add some shading, and this baby elephant is ready to go.

Golden Retriever Puppy

The golden retriever puppy is one of the most popular breeds of dog in the world. Highly intelligent and eager to please, it is very easy to train. This active puppy likes to swim and play, but mostly it just loves to be around its human companions.

2 Next, sketch in the legs. The paws will start out as ovals and be adjusted later. Next, add the tail and start sketching the pup's face.

1 Start out with these simple shapes to help define the proportions of the dog.

4 Your puppy is almost complete. Add some golden color and shading, and your puppy is ready to play catch!

3 Tighten up your drawing by adding muscle tone and details. At this stage, you can add finer details such as fur and whiskers.

American Short Hair Kitten

Cute and cuddly, the American short hair kitten comes in many different colors and over 80 patterns. It was first brought over to America on the Mayflower in order to chase down the rats aboard the ship. Gentle and playful, this kitten gets along well with people and even dogs.

2 Draw the hind and front legs as shown. Then, sketch in ovals for the paws. Now that the main body is planned out, you can begin to add smaller details such as the ears, eyes and mouth.

1 Start by sketching two large ovals for the body and then connect them, as shown. Then, draw a large circle for the head. Next, draw a smaller oval for the nose and mouth area.

 Add some light shading for a 3-D effect and your kitten will be complete.

3 Your kitten is nearly finished. Start refining the details on the ears and paws, as well as adding fur and the tail. Erase any unwanted guidelines.

Lamb

A baby lamb can identify its mother by the distinctive "bleat" sound she makes. The lamb stays with its mother until it is six months old. Then it is considered to be fully grown. A one-year old sheep is called a hogget and a two-year old sheep is called a two-tooth.

2 Now, add the lamb's lower limbs. Pencil in the small hooves. Then, add the ears and plan out the face by sketching in the mouth, nose, and eyes.

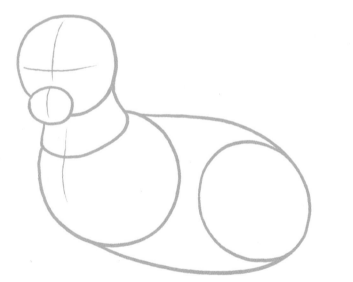

1 Draw the baby lamb lying down. First, draw a circular shape for the head and a smaller circle for the muzzle. Then, draw the neck. Draw two more circles and connect them, as shown.

4 Your sketch is nearly complete. Add some soft shading to make your lamb look real.

3 Once all the main parts are drawn out, start adding the fine details to the ears, face, and body.

Giraffe Calf

The baby of one of the tallest animals that lives on land, a giraffe calf is about six feet tall when born. The coat pattern on each giraffe calf is unique. When the calf's mother goes off to feed, it is left with other young giraffes in a place known as a "calving ground." Once older, it will join its mother.

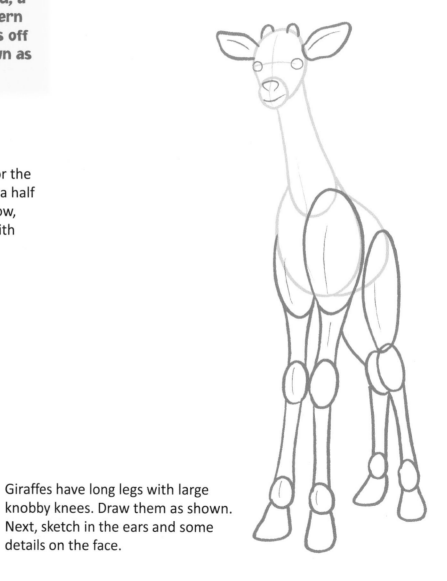

1 Start with a medium size oval for the main part of the body. Connect a half circle to create the hind end. Now, draw the long neck. Top it off with two ovals, as shown.

2 Giraffes have long legs with large knobby knees. Draw them as shown. Next, sketch in the ears and some details on the face.

14

4 Once you add some color and shading, your giraffe will be ready to eat leaves off of tall trees.

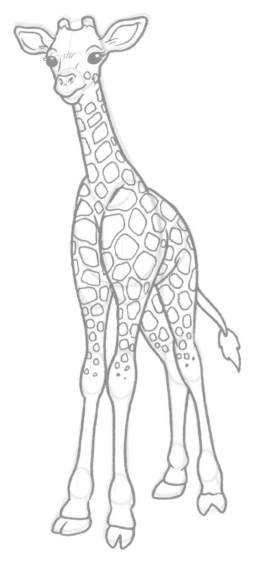

3 Now you can sketch more details. Add the tail and the spots. Erase any unwanted guidelines.

Grizzly Bear Cubs

The grizzly bear cub is usually born with a twin during the winter season while its mother is hibernating. Cubs are taken very well care of by their mother, who will fiercely defend them if she thinks they are in danger. Very energetic, the cubs love to play and jump on one another.

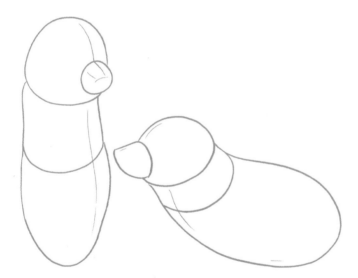

1 Start with the main body shapes, as shown. Then, sketch in the head shapes.

2 Draw the two bears' limbs. One will be in a standing pose on its two hind legs and the other will be on all four paws. Now, add the ear shapes and plan out the eye shapes.

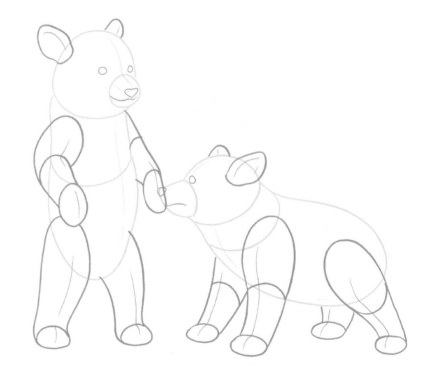

3 Once your initial sketches look how you want, add more detail to the bears' faces. At this point, add the the whiskers and fur detail.

4 Add shading to the cubs. Now, they are ready to play with each other in a cool stream.

Piglet

A baby pig, also known as a piglet, is a very clean, intelligent, and social animal. Some are born with curly tails and others with straight tails. Piglets like to snuggle close together when resting and use grunts to communicate with one another. Since piglets don't have sweat glands, they cool off by rolling around in the mud.

2 Use these simple shapes to sketch in the legs. Now, add the big ears.

1 This piglet sketch will start with these simple shapes. Once you have the head shape worked out, you can add the snout.

4 Add some lighting and shading to give your piggy some depth. He's ready to roll around in mud!

3 Now, add some final details in the ears, add wrinkles, and splayed hooves. Erase any unwanted guidelines.

Spaniel Puppy

This sweet pup is very friendly, affectionate, and loves to cuddle. Curious by nature, the Spaniel truly enjoys the outdoors where it is able to run around and explore its surroundings. This pup is easy to train because, not only is it very intelligent, but it also likes to be part of the family.

2 Now that you have the basic shape sketched, you can sketch in the puppy's tail, legs, and paws. Then, add the ears and begin to detail the rest of the puppy's face.

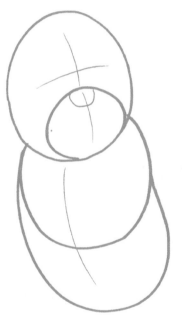

1 This cute puppy starts out with these simple shapes. The top oval will be his head; lightly pencil in the nose and muzzle shapes.

4 Once your puppy sketch is finished, add color and shading to really bring your drawing to life. Your Spaniel is ready for adventure!

3 Add important details like the pup's fur, whiskers, and tongue. Keep adding little details until your puppy looks complete.

Calf

A calf weighs about 40 pounds at birth and can see, stand, and walk when born. Cows have an incredible sense of smell and can detect an odor up to six miles away. Calves are fed milk until they are about nine weeks old. A female calf will grow up to be a cow. A male calf will become a bull.

2 Add the front and hind legs. When drawing the hooves, make them slightly pointy at the ends. Then, add the ears, horns, and face.

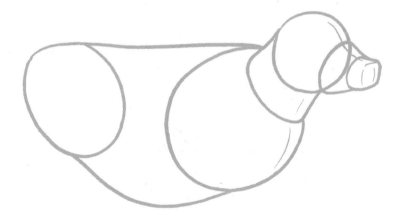

1 Begin sketching the calf with these simple shapes for the body. Next, add the snout.

 You are ready for color. Add some shading and highlighting, and this calf is ready to graze.

3 This calf is ready for more details. Sketch the tail and give the face more definition. Don't forget to erase any unwanted guidelines.

Chick

As soon as a chick can breathe, it can also peep. It needs much warmth for the first few weeks of its life until its feathers appear. A chick loves to be gently petted. At the age of six months, a female chick, now called a hen, will begin laying eggs.

2 Next, add the wing shape. Sketch in the two legs, as shown. Lightly sketch in the eye shape and start to define the beak.

1 Baby chicks can be drawn by using only a few simple shapes. Start with a large oval for the body, as shown. Then, draw the head shape with a simple beak.

 Add some color or shading to complete. This little chick is ready to explore the farm!

3 Now is the fun part. Add some fluff to the chick's body and finish off the leg details.

Horse Foal

A foal can walk, trot, and run just a couple of hours after being born. About a week later, a foal will cut its first tooth. Until the age of three, male foals are referred to as colts and female foals as fillies.

2 Now, draw the horse's legs. Each leg has two main circles where they bend. Draw those circles first and connect them, as shown. Sketch in the ears and eye placement.

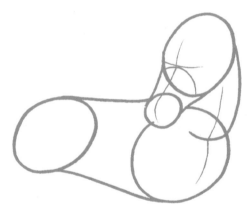

1 Draw two ovals, as shown, and connect them for the body. Then, draw the head shape with a long muzzle. Add the neck.

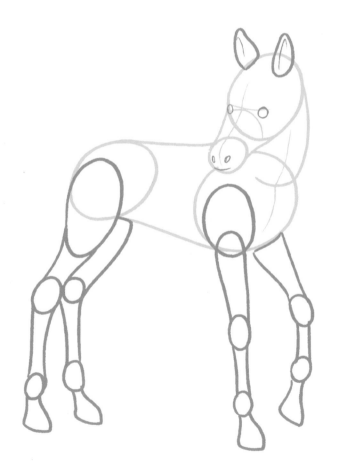

 Add some color shading to the sketch for dimension. Your foal is ready to trot off to a grassy meadow.

3 Next, add some finer detail like the foal's tail. Add some muscle tone and finish the facial details. Then, erase any unwanted guidelines.

Abyssinian Kitten

An Abyssinian kitten is very independent, loves to play with water, and has a very quiet "purr." Believed to be one of the oldest breeds in the world, this kitten has tons of energy and loves to jump onto high places. Its coat can come in several different colors.

2 Draw the kitten's hind and front legs. Add the paws by drawing small ovals. Next, draw the ears like rounded triangles on the head. Start defining the nose and mouth area, and pencil in circles for the eyes.

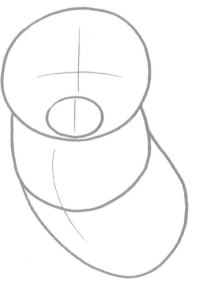

1 This cat starts out with a large oval for the head. Find the center of the head oval and add a smaller oval at the bottom. Next, draw the body by connecting the shapes.

 Once you have a solid pose, start adding important details that will finish the sketch. Now, add the fur and whiskers.

4 You can use colored pencils or markers to add shading to finalize it.

Emperor Penguin Chick

The emperor penguin chick cannot fly when born and has very soft gray feathers called down. At about six weeks, the emperor penguin chick will join other chicks in a crèche (a place where chicks are taken care of during the day, by other adult penguins). As the chick grows older, its feathers turn black and white.

2 Next, sketch in the wings and rough shapes for his eyes, beak, and toes.

1 Penguins start out life pretty fluffy. First, sketch out these three shapes. This will look like a snowman.

 Add some shading and this little penguin is all set to waddle around.

 Now, add some detail to its face, then some pencil marks to indicate its fluffy feathers.

Fawn

A baby deer, known as a fawn, is able to stand and walk shortly after birth. When young, it does not have any scent, which helps to protect it against predators. The fawn's coat is reddish brown with small white spots. These spots disappear at about five months after birth when it gets its first winter coat.

2 Add the long legs, using these basic shapes. Note the shape of the hooves.

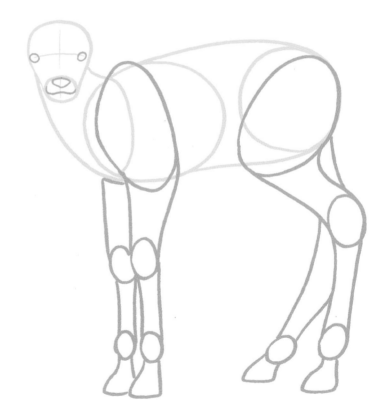

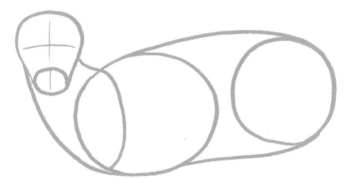

1 Start with an oval and a smaller circle. Connect them to create the body. Draw the head and neck shapes, as shown.

 Add some soft shading to finalize your sketch. Add lighter fur spots to the fawn's back. The fawn looks ready to play in the forest.

 Now, add its ears and tail. Then, finish off the fine details by adding fur and muscle lines. Erase unwanted guidelines.

Chimpanzee

A baby chimp is very curious and loves to play with friends (other chimps) and explore its surroundings. It also loves to be groomed and go for rides on its mother's back.

2 Now, draw the legs and arms. Chimps have human-like hands. Take note of the fingers' shapes. Add the ears and slightly pencil in the face.

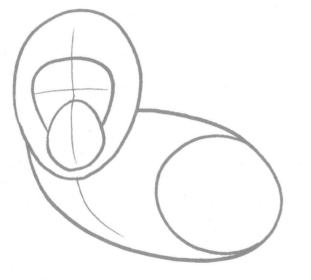

1 Begin sketching a large oval for the body. Draw another oval for the head. Then, start planning out the face.

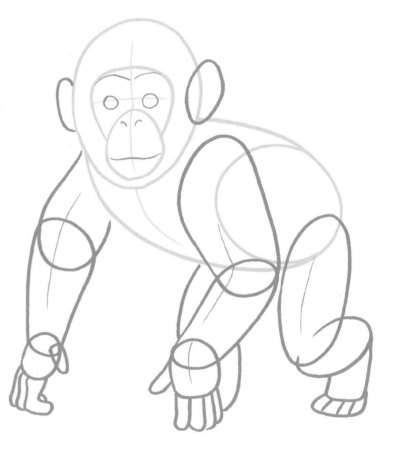

4 Add some color shading, and soon your chimp will be swinging from tree to tree.

 Finish your chimp sketch by adding some fur and more facial detail.

Hippopotamus Calf

A hippo calf knows how to swim right away because it is born under water. The calf produces pink-colored oil that helps keep its skin moist in the heat. The calf spends most of its days in the water or wallowing in the mud, and comes on land in the evening to graze on grass.

2 Sketch in the front and back legs. Add the hippo's ears and sketch in the eye positions.

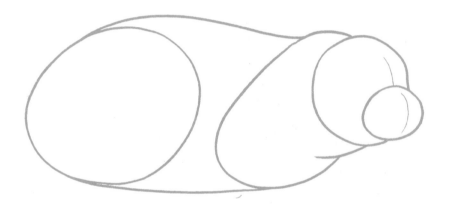

1 Start by drawing the body and head shape, as shown.

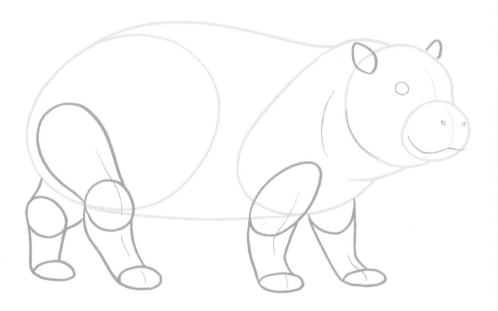

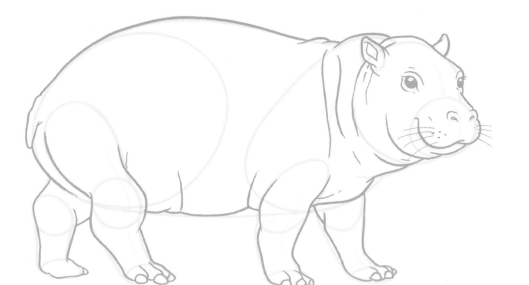

4 Next, add some shading and this hippo is ready to wallow in the mud.

3 To finalize your sketch, add some wrinkles and skin folds. Then, draw in the whiskers.

Zebra Foal

A zebra foal is able to stand and walk shortly after being born—just like its distant relative, the horse. Each zebra's stripes are different from every other zebra's—no two zebras are the same. When a zebra foal is born, it has brown stripes. By adulthood, the brown stripes have turned black.

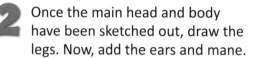 Once the main head and body have been sketched out, draw the legs. Now, add the ears and mane.

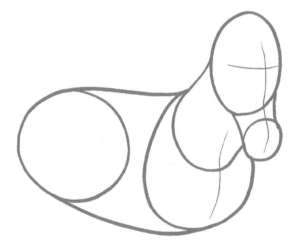

1 Start by drawing an oval for the head, then draw another smaller oval for the muzzle. Then, connect them. Next, draw the body shape, as shown.

Add some shading. This zebra foal can head off for a fun gallop.

3 Finalize the details by adding muscle tone. Then, add the many stripes on the zebra's skin and mane. Erase any guidelines.

Leopard Cub

The leopard cub is kept hidden in a hollow tree trunk or dense bush until it is about six to eight weeks old. By this time, it can already climb trees and eat solid food that its mother brings to it. A cub stays with its mother for almost two years and then it is ready to go off into the wild on its own.

2 Add the front and back legs, as shown. Then, add ovals for the paws. Sketch in the ears and tail. Also, lightly pencil in the eyes and mouth.

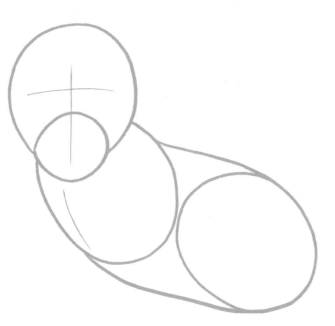

1 Draw two large ovals for the body and connect them. Then, draw a large circle for the head and another small circle for the muzzle.

3 Define the detail of the face and paws. Add whiskers and sketch in the many spots.

4 Next, add color and shading. This cub is ready to explore.

Harp Seal Pup

The harp seal pup is born with silky snow-white fur. This beautiful fur sheds when it is about three weeks old. It is called a "ragged jacket" during this time. Before it learns how to swim, the pup is referred to as a "beater" because it beats the surface.

2 Next, add the front and back limbs, which are used to swim in the water. Lightly sketch in the nose and eye circles.

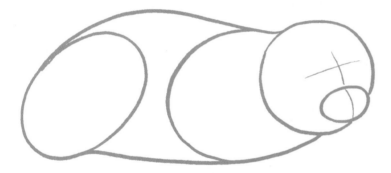

1 Start with a few slanted ovals and connect them for the body. Then, draw in a few circles for the head, as shown.

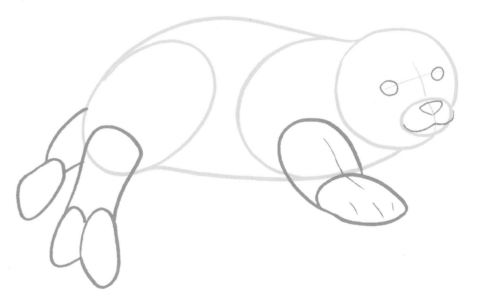

4 With a graphite or colored pencil, add some texture to the fur with some light shading. This pup is ready for a dive!

3 Begin to finalize this pup by adding details, such as the whiskers and wrinkles. Erase any unwanted guidelines.

Koala "Joey"

A baby koala, referred to as a "joey" (like a baby kangaroo), is born bald, blind, and very tiny. It then crawls into its mother's pouch and stays there for the next six months. During this time, it will only drink its mother's milk. Once it gets older, it will begin to eat eucalyptus leaves and ride on its mother's back. A joey usually leaves its mother when it is about 18 months old.

2 Next, sketch in the legs and arms. Add the large ears. Then, sketch in the toes and fingers.

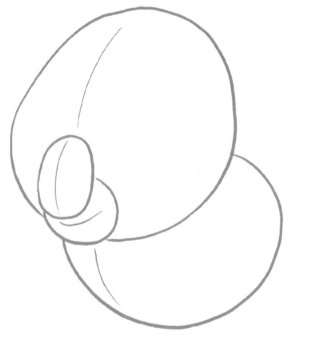

1 Start with two large oval shapes. Then, add two ovals for the mouth and nose.

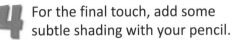
4 For the final touch, add some subtle shading with your pencil.

3 Once the main shapes have been sketched, add some additional details such as fur. Erase any unwanted guidelines.

Dolphin Calf

The minute a dolphin calf is born, the mother helps it to the surface of the water, so it can take its first breath. The calf is taken great care of by its mother for the first four years. Each dolphin has its own unique whistle that distinguishes it from other dolphins.

1 Begin with a large oval and add a long tail. Next, sketch a small oval for the beak.

2 Add the dorsal fin to the back and the flipper to the side. Also, add the tail fin.

 Slightly shade the dolphin to give the illusion of depth. This dolphin is ready to swim.

3 Next, add subtle details around the flipper and eye.

Lion Cub

A lion cub is born blind—its eyes do not open until a week after birth. A young cub grows quickly and, in just a week, it may double its body weight. In the early months of its life, a cub explores its surroundings by play fighting with others. It must learn how to hunt and fend for itself by the age of two. At this time, the female becomes the hunter and stays with the pride—the male searches for its own pride.

2 Add the legs as shown and small circles for the paws.

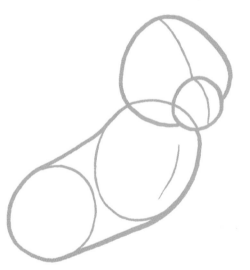

1 Sketch an oval with two circles within it for the body. Next, draw a circle for the head and a smaller circle for the muzzle.

4 Color in your cub and add some shading and highlighting to give depth to the fur.

3 Add the ears, tail, and facial details. Erase any unwanted lines.

Orangutan

A baby orangutan is constantly carried by its mother for the first year. The baby stays with its mother until it's about seven years old. During this time, the mother teaches her baby what food to eat and where to find it, so that it is ready to live on its own.

2 Now, draw the legs and arms. Add the ears and continue to detail the face.

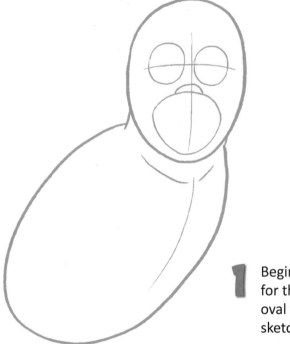

1 Begin by drawing a large oval for the body. Draw another oval for the head and lightly sketch in the face shapes.

 Add some color shading to complete this cute drawing.

3 Finish your orangutan sketch by adding some fur and hand details. Erase any unwanted guidelines.

Panda Bear Cub

A panda bear cub is born blind and weighs no more than four ounces. By the time it turns six months old, the cub is already eating its food of choice—bamboo. This is also the age when its mother stops taking care of it. Pandas can spend about 16 hours a day eating bamboo (the leaves, shoots, and stems).

2 Sketch the limbs, tail, and ears. Now, draw in the eyes and plan out the face.

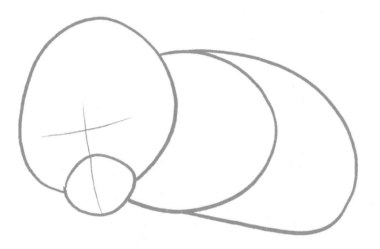

1 Start with an oval for the head and sketch in a circle for the muzzle. Then, add the round body, as shown.

4 Add some shading to indicate the darker parts on the bear. This cub is ready for fun.

3 With the main body parts of your panda sketched out, add in the details, such as the fur.

Rabbit Kitten

A baby rabbit, known as a kitten, is born in a nest made by its mother. In order to stay safe from predators, the baby will burrow beneath the nest and only come out when being fed milk by its mother. These feedings usually occur once a day for the first eight weeks of its life. By then, it is able to eat solid food.

2 Next, draw in the bunny's legs and tail. Then, sketch in the ear shapes. Slightly pencil in the face details.

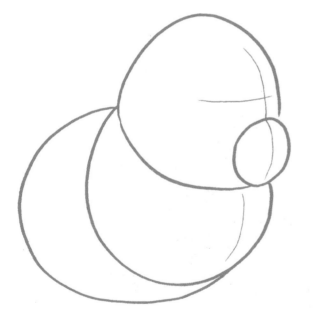

1 Sketch in the head and body shapes, as shown.

 Once your bunny sketch is finished, add color and shading to really bring the drawing to life.

 Add some final details to the fur, face, and paws. Erase any unwanted guidelines.

Raccoon Kit

This raccoon kit (or cub, as it is also called) is very helpless as a newborn. It does not open its eyes until about three weeks old. By the time it is seven weeks old, this kit will walk, play, and climb with other raccoon kits. This nocturnal mammal (active at night) will begin to go out at night with its mother when it is about three months old. Until that time, it will stay back in its family den.

2 Next, draw in the limbs and tail. Add the ears. Now, draw in the mask on the raccoon's face.

1 Start with a circle for the head and sketch in the muzzle. Then, add the neck and body, as shown.

4 Next, add some shading to make the baby raccoon look more realistic. It's off to find some food!

3 With the main parts sketched out, add some fur details. Then, sketch in the rings on the tail.

Cheetah Cub

Born blind, a cheetah cub is unable to walk until it is about 15 days old. The cub is protected, fed, and taught how to hunt and survive in the wild by its mother. When the mother feels the cub can take care of itself—usually at about 18 months of age—she will abandon it while it sleeps.

1 Draw two large ovals for the body and connect them. Then, draw a large circle for the head and another small circle for the muzzle.

2 Add the front and back legs, as shown. Then, add ovals for the paws. Sketch in the ears and tail. Also, lightly pencil in the eyes and mouth.

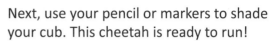 Next, use your pencil or markers to shade your cub. This cheetah is ready to run!

3 Define the detail of the face and paws. Add some whiskers and then sketch in the many spots. Erase any unwanted guidelines.

Gray Wolf Puppy

A gray wolf puppy is born deaf and blind. It is taken care of by its mother and other members of the pack. As the pup grows, it is very active and loves to play with its brothers and sisters. After a few months, the puppy is ready to run and hunt with the rest of the pack.

2 Draw in the front and hind legs. Add the tail and sketch in the ears. Lightly pencil in the eyes, nose, and mouth.

1 Draw an oval shape for the head and add the muzzle. Next, draw the neck and body shapes, as shown.

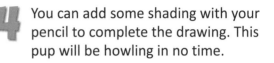

4 You can add some shading with your pencil to complete the drawing. This pup will be howling in no time.

3 Finalize your sketch by adding some fur. Also, add some details to the paws and face, including whiskers.

Owlet

A baby owl, known as an owlet, remains in its nest for about six weeks after being born. It begins to take flight at seven weeks and can fly very well by about ten weeks. To see in different directions, it must turn its head around because its eyes are fixed in their sockets.

2 Pencil in the wings and feet shapes. Next, pencil in the large eyes and beak shape.

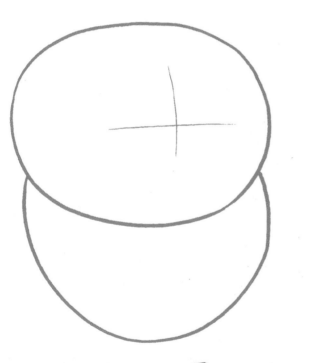

1 Draw a large oval for the head and then another for the body.

3 Now that the main parts have been sketched out, add some final touches like feathers. Erase any unwanted guidelines.

4 Next, add color and shading. This owlet is ready for a fun night.